The Werewolf Doesn't Die in the End

C. ANNE GARDNER

A SEVEN7H TANGENT BOOK

ILLUSTRATIONS

Cover "Death" by Martin Whitmore (martinwhitmore.com)
"The Fool" by RoseJean Weller
"The Moon" by Rachael Smith, C. Anne Gardner & Martin Whitmore
"Strength" by Amber Romano & Martin Whitmore
"The Sun" by Cadence McCracken

Book Design by J. Brandon Loberg
Set in Mercury, Ideal Sans, and Mezalia

Published by SEVEN7H TANGENT in San Francisco, CA
ISBN: 979-8-234-03514-1

FIRST PRINTING

THE STORY

A Glossary of Terms

Lycanthrope

Creatures that usually present as human, however will transform into a wolf-like creature at the rise of the full moon. Usually, werewolves are considered dangerous, or even deadly. Most commonly, lycanthropes are the result of a curse, being bitten by another werewolf, or being born as a werewolf.

Medical Trauma

When an individual has experienced trauma as the result of a medical condition or medical treatment. This can also be the result of a lack of proper medical care.

Mental Illness

Any condition that causes changes in thinking, emotion, or behavior; this must be significant enough to cause regular distress in the sufferer's daily life and their ability to perform activities to meet the criteria for diagnosis.

Neurodivergence

The state of living with a brain that functions differently from the majority population, leading to notable differences in how individuals think, feel, learn, and behave.

Post-Traumatic Stress Disorder (PTSD)

A disorder that causes significant, ongoing distress following an acute traumatic event. If the trauma has been ongoing for an extended period of time, the diagnosis is more commonly referred to as Complex Post-Traumatic Stress Disorder (C-PTSD).

Premenstrual Dysphoric Disorder (PMDD)

A neuroendocrine condition that causes an abnormal neurological response to the normal hormonal changes of the menstrual cycle. This response is often severe in nature, and causes major psychological and behavioral issues in the luteal phase of the menstrual cycle, most of which typically subside at the onset of menstruation. This disorder is both poorly studied and historically under-diagnosed, with most sufferers waiting roughly fifteen years to receive a proper diagnosis. According to the Journal of Affective Disorders, thirty-four percent of PMDD sufferers have attempted suicide.

*Follow your inner moonlight;
don't hide the madness.*

ALLEN GINSBERG

Forward

i was bitten by a werewolf // a potential i once thought // only existed in fairy tales // i did not believe // that there was something inside of me // that would eat me alive // until i felt dead // long before my time // i have heard the stories of the others // of witches who perceive what no one else can // sirens who sing while they are drowning // oracles who predict catastrophe while bearing the weight of knowledge // shapeshifters who become reflections with no shadow of their own // ghosts who float through the worlds of both the here and gone // vampires who bleed everyone close to them dry // poltergeists who whisper disaster into being // genies trapped in body-shaped bottles that crack and shatter // but never release // little girls who are told they are cursed from the beginning // little boys forced to shoulder the world unflinchingly // like titans // too many creatures to count // which is why no one really has yet // sometimes // the monster is all in their heads // sometimes // their bones // blood // muscles // phantom limbs // the past // the future // no one can find it // but they know it is *somewhere* // because it is *something* that looks like a beast // talks like a man // croons like a requiem // and bites like the tip of a poisoned blade // over three-hundred moons ago i was bitten by a werewolf // i didn't know it then // the only sign: a pool of blood // an empty void // then claw marks // slashing // marking // and tallying // eras // they say that everyone changes // that innocence always ends in revolution // and hopefully a triumphant finish // but i never stopped evolving // moonrise after moonrise // and only in the direction of glory // once i found the daybreak // digging my nails into cavern walls // painted with violence // and strife // and a story emerged // that repeated // and repeated // until it was no longer mine // but could be anyone's // from this point forward

Hero

Heroes do not exist.
Neither do Villains,

because all dichotomies die
in the process of becoming.

This is not a story of villainy
any more than it is the parable
of "First they came for us…"

because then, they came for themselves
and each other, gnawing at extremities,
seeking the origin of the wound.

People are not wounds.
They are not salves.
They are not saviors
any more than they are
fauna in constant flux.

Do not perceive me Hero.
Do not outline me Enemy
or analyze me Protagonist.

I am a sculpture of shoulder chips.
A catalyst, agonist, turning point
for some greater god, forged in
a lesser-known minor arcana mythology.

I've journeyed how Atlas journeyed:
the downfall inevitable and the world
forever agony-heavy. Hubris has
shown me to its Hell and back again

but this is what mortals do:
build their bibles on the shoulders
of the same plots they've conquered
and name their trials "Other"
in order to remain in the light.

Survival is not a happy ending
any more than it is a tragedy.
Survivors can die as easily
as anyone racing bullets
and outpacing destiny.

I am not asking you to write
an ode to my triumph
or the triumphant —
to etch my name
into the marble of history.

My story is a needle
significance is a haystack
and suffering is every farm in Kansas

but maybe the razored hunger
ground thanklessly into golden fleece
deserves to be bound by something other
than a pair of flimsy plastic bookends.

I left footprints that shine under moonlight:
a troubled track that traces all at once
a map, a farewell, a testimony, and a fable.

I am not the Hero of this story;
I couldn't be, even if I wanted to

but this story is full of so many heroes
that the greatest tragedy ever written
would be one that remains untold.

WAXING

Shadows

I grew up in a village
shrouded in mystery.
I began by whispering
to anyone who would listen
that it isn't safe outside.

That is where the wolves are.

I began to believe
what I was told about myself —
that I made monsters of men.

So I reached fingers out
like olive branches
vying to touch something soft.

When I brought back bite marks
I must have scraped my hands
climbing fences. I must have
chewed off my own nails.

When they asked me who did it
I cried *Wolf,* so *of course*

no one believed me.

How ungrateful I am
for not blessing all these sheep
in my pasture. There is something
not right with me. I must have
blurry vision. I must choose
to have nightmares over dreams.

I should have ignored their howling
like it was my own.

Not Normal

A baby cries because it is hungry.

A toddler begs for another hour's play.
Spits out the dinner plate's broccoli.
Throws a tantrum in the candy aisle.

A child falls off their two-wheel
scrapes a knee, and wails
until the Band-Aid arrives.

An adolescent yells at their mother,
tired of the cloister of household rules.
Sneaks sips of communion wine.

Siblings fight over shared toys
or grieve when the family pet dies.
They compete to be favorite.

Bodies react. Bodies feel.
Bodies want and need and bleed...

...and bodies change, grow
and move in mysterious ways.

All of this is normal

but when
a young girl snatches a kitchen knife
pressing to her throat while her eyes
turn an unfamiliar shade of amber

this is not normal

innocence rising to emergency
and flipping on a too-bright siren.

Not misguided ploy any more
than it is trauma's familiar wail

it blooms with a strange gravity —

the desire to slice chalk outlines
into the skin's most fragile pavement

fear coaxing out the fervor.

The same child wakes the next morning
understanding she transformed
into something unrecognizable.

The body reacted too much.
The body felt too deeply.

The body unflinchingly resolved
that self-destruction tasted sweet.

The body changed too quickly
for anyone to sound the alarm.
To call this sickness. To say

this is not normal

but everyone told her it was

so I thought it was

for so much longer than
should have been normal.

Episode

when asked
to describe
an episode

there is
no meaning,
only feeling
and sound like

> *gullet shorn*
> *mask bladed*
> *fire throat*
> *death weave*
> *twist tail*
> *clot ridden*
> *error farm*
> *pit of hell*
> *gutted, glazed*
> *lapping poison*
> *thieving chainmail*
> *endless dice roll*
> *undead, unseen*
> *flickering patience*
> *dungeon shuttered*

> *loud loud loud*

and then gone —
like a distant
and whispering
swarm of nails

Frog in Boiling Water

When the pot boils over
and I become hot-headed
purgatorial amphibian...

I try my best to stay inside.
To swallow the scalpel —
like it isn't an act of violence,
but a more palatable one.

What is tolerable must be living.
What stings must still be growth.
I have trained myself to ignore
the rising ebb of discomfort

breath leaving,
chest becoming bellows,
anxiety slowly slipping up
the ladder of thermometer ticks
until solace seems just nearly reachable...

They say the frog doesn't notice —
if it is comfortable enough,
the heat can be managed...
put out of mind...

until the mind begs
to be put out of misery.

This is the wives' tale, of course.
Some frogs notice they are wilting,
trying everything to save themselves

unlike humans, who willingly perish
to escape the reach of hungry hands.
That room temperature combustion

because it is not being burned alive
that scares us most.

It is continuing to live like this.

Perfectly Fine

In rehab, the doctor tells me
that my downfall was "explosive."

What he means is that
my stint with substances
was short and loud
as much as it seemed
so effortlessly defused.

I am fifteen.
Addiction pulled me in like
a siren's song for the sailor
who was not just alone at sea,
but already drowning.

This is an off-key aria
yelling fire in an empty room,
because there were years
I couldn't understand the ways
in which I pulled my own pins.

This is the flooded ruin
of this body. This is
the misdiagnosis of "troubled."
This is the cautionary tale
of what happens when
there is a ticking in your stomach
and the clock is running back
and everyone still tells you
that you are *perfectly fine*.

Years later I see bodies
bent into sidewalk half-folds
or playing dead under awnings.
I visit the graves of friends.
I step between needles
like cracks in the concrete
breaking their mothers' hearts.

I wonder what shrapnel
is still lodged in their spines.
Which neurons burst in silence.
Which doctor or badge or judge
sent them away to detonate
in a forest of already fallen trees.

I was once a pile of powder
next to an open flame,
but I was also a cracked carapace
reassembled by careful hands.

There are parts of me
that will always be fractured —
moth-flutter in the direction of dying light —

and I won't be the first, or last
to burn out in pursuit of betterment.

Still, I consider myself lucky —

Too many of us
will spend our whole lives
as smoke.

Chicken or the Egg

I don't know which came first:
the trauma or the disorder.
The jackhammer heartbeat
courting the fear of crumbling

or the snapped bridge cables
between strands of my composure
that left a trip-wire where veins
could have fed some certainty.

It is a vicious moon cycle:
the beginning chasing the ending
chasing the new beginning, meanwhile
growing all the more tired of endings.

I remember the first time my blood
curdled from beneath the surface.
I remember that it burned so badly
that no one could quiet the seethe.

It wasn't always this.

I was once a child swallowing
the knots in my throat. Or laughing
so loudly that skinned knees dulled.

I do not know which came first:
the loneliness or what caused it.
If the hydrant burst from the pressure
or was struck in an accidental swerve.

All I know is that now there is a flood
that everyone runs from. I stanch it
with eggshells, kicking them into voids
when it's too late to evacuate alone.

I have slaughtered a henhouse of birds.
Somehow their offspring keep hatching.

What is the most original mistake?

What the world has done to me?
Or what I have done to it —

this downward spiral of chromosomes
asking to be named something other
than a flock of night terrors.

I have always had words
for chickens and eggs: for the terms
cascading down prescription labels

but until I know the origin of their births —
or if they too are wolves leaving the cages
slaughtered and emptied each morning —

there are gaps that may never seal
and parables I may never understand, like

What came first? Me or what made me?
The birth or the birds? The Garden of Eden
or the evolution charting its downfall?

This fragile shell of a body?
Or how afraid it is
of what it could someday become?

A List of Synonyms

WEREWOLF (cont.)

Abusive

Angry

Asshole

Bipolar

Bitch

Borderline

Crazy

Daniel "Oz" Osborne

David Kessler

Disabled

Draugluin

Emotional

Explosive

Fenrir Greyback

Fluffy

Hugh Jackman

Hysterical

Intense

Irrational

Jacob Black

James Howlett

King Lycaon

Lawrence Talbot

Logan

Loup-garou

Lost cause

Lycanthrope

Mentally Ill

Monster

Moody

Neurodivergent

Overreacting

PMSing

Psycho

Remus Lupin

Scott McCall

Taylor Lautner

Traumatized

Uncontrollable

Unlovable

Unwell

Versipellis

Wolfen

Wolf Man

Wolverine

*Why was I given so many names
that only ever made it harder
for me to find my own?*

Enter the Werewolf

This transformation is an optical illusion:
every sharp and incomparable thing
distorted, twisting in a funhouse mirror
like water in the desert, disappearing
the moment you arrive at its edge.

Imagine that you are your own gaslight.

Imagine waking up from a nightmare
that lasts all day, only to be amazed
that none of it was real because you swore
you felt the hands tightening closed
around your throat, the sky
clouding with ash, spitting lightning
that somehow never touched the ground.

The body becomes cloaked in phantoms.
When resisted, they threaten to invade.
To possess. To breathe ice and terror
down the spine, swallowing it whole.

Consumption always ends in bloodshed,
each rise at dusk bringing the omen:
that familiar approaching shadow, but

in the morning, every staircase
in the Escher painting of yesterday
magically leads to firm landings.
Everything suddenly makes sense...

...except for the vacant rooms.
The gashes carved into doorframes.
Bruises, holes, and battle scars.
Signs of violence. Blood spatters
lining blue walls of incoherent text

and the absence of friends, lovers, family
torn to shreds in the wake of something
that feels distant and impossible
the moment the sunrise breaks.

All of us have killed something beautiful
or worry we might still, because
we recognize our own reflections.
Cower from them most of the time

but we are not monsters any more
than we are running from the monsters.

Sometimes we pray for the Huntsman
or turn to witch doctors peddling poison,
even haggling with the Devil himself

because we'd sell our souls to only ever be
the person we see on the good days:
desperate and tired of becoming
bared teeth and down on all fours

even when the curse lifts easily enough
and all we can reclaim in its absence is that

this transformation is an optical illusion:
every sharp and incomparable thing
distorted, twisting in a funhouse mirror
like water in the desert, disappearing
when the wanderer reaches its edge.

We chase solace in circles like this —
lost boys running from shadows
following half-eaten breadcrumbs

while always on vigilant lookout
for a fantastic half-human menace
emerging from a cautionary tale
beneath a moon no one else can see.

FULL

XVIII
FULL

The Village

In the olden days, they called it Witchcraft.
At the birth of medicine, they called it Hysteria.
Frankenstein's creation was called Monster.
In the 50s it was the Communists.
In the 80s it was the Queers.

Something to blame: a name
for the bane of the village

because simplicity sees what is easiest
in the only language it knows,
like children who call all animals   *dog*
because they haven't yet learned   *deer*

Sometimes I look at them and wonder
who they would have been in the past
The voice of reason? The bystander?

History does not repeat itself well
when the sanctuary shuns its margins
in the back-turning enclaves of the world.
Fortresses mislabeled as communities
have body counts falling into backlogs.

A court of small nobles chug mead,
spit out empathy like spoiled milk,
mistake biases for boundaries,
and refuse to expand borders
in the name of a growing kingdom.

But the village is Able
entitled and carefree.
Everything else is the dark
mysterious beyond.

Misunderstanding is called illness
in a society that believes
if we ourselves become sick
the doctor will *of course* find a cure.

What a rude awakening it is to learn
that it is cheaper and more convenient
to disappear into the arms of obscurity
when fresh air and an afternoon class
are not enough to induce assimilation.

How cursed is this town to have an outcast!
How lucky are the pariahs to avoid the blight!
They don't have to sweep themselves from view!

When asking anyone why
they can't *just be okay*
doesn't magically make them okay,
we all stop believing in our history
and start believing in Hysteria, because

there is something wrong in the village:
a lethal concoction of caution
superstition and revised history.

"Be careful" it says, turning all
the mirrors. *"If you look in one*
you might just see your own shadow."

If You Lived With a Werewolf

If you lived with a werewolf
what would you do?
Would you buy them some gloves
and a big pair of shoes?

Would they join you for dinner?
Would they sleep in a cage?
Would you slip them a tonic
to soften their rage?

When the moon came up full,
would you lock all the doors?
Shutter the windows?
Seal the holes in the floors?

In the morning would you let them
crawl back on their knees?
When they said they were sorry
would you be appeased?

If you lived with a werewolf
just part of the time,
would you ever forgive them?
Would you ever be kind?

Or did you ever love them?
Feel the heartbeat through fur?
Would that lost soul deserve
the fate they incur?

If the villagers told you
there was nothing worth saving,
would you remember their thirst
was a curse, not a craving?

Would you hide silver bullets
under the bed?
Wait til they were sleeping
to shoot for the head?

When you both realized
it was kill or be killed
would you spill the first blood?
Watch them fall, then lie still?

And when they turned back
and you looked in their eyes,
would the emptiness feel
like a fair compromise?

If you lived with a werewolf
would you remember before
they changed into something
you could only abhor?

Would you mourn what was lost?
Embrace what was gained?
Was saving them a mission
you once entertained?

If you hunted the thing
that was once a life,
would you regret every moment
you sharpened your knife?

If you lived with a werewolf,
what would you do?
Would you know the outcome?
Have the faintest clue?

And when it was certain
just what would come true,
would you ever ask why
they chose to die with you?

Howl

1.

Wolves howl because they are trying
to communicate. To reach others
who are a part of their pack. Often
they howl to gather in one location.
To mark where they are and what they own
so that they can be most easily found.

Howls are honest. A desire for the sky
to unveil emergency broadcast beacon.

Sometimes howls indicate sadness.
A longing. A need or cry for help,
but most often it is information.
A plea expressed as a soliloquy.

Wolf Howl:

I just wanted you to know that things are so hard right now.
I see you and all I can think about is how difficult this has
become. I just want it all to be different.

I'm sorry, but I don't know if I can keep this up. I'm so fucking
tired all the time and everything seems like too much. I wish
this wasn't such a burden on you, but I can't make you understand
why I am always angry at myself for never being what you need.

2.

When a village has been plagued
by a werewolf, every howl is a warning
that the beast is coming for them.

They do not imagine that it is searching
for family, or home; only blood, violence
or mutually assured destruction.

Werewolf Howl:

> I JUST wanted YOU to KNOW that things are SO HARD RIGHT NOW.
> I see YOU and ALL I CAN THINK ABOUT is how DIFFICULT THIS HAS
> BECOME. I JUST want it ALL to be DIFFERENT.

> I'm SORRY, but I DON'T KNOW if I can KEEP doing THIS. I'm so FUCKING
> tired ALL THE TIME and EVERYTHING seems like it is TOO MUCH. I wish
> this wasn't such a BURDEN ON YOU, but I can't make YOU UNDERSTAND
> why I am ALWAYS ANGRY at MYSELF for NEVER being what YOU need.

3.

In ancient tales, werewolves
rarely travel in packs,
so often alone on cliffsides —
the moon their sole companion.

They beg for sunrise to approach.
To pull them into some new gravity.

Though howls are designed as claims —
in a long-forgotten language
of sounds arranged into maps —
they're most often received as snarls:
signals to prepare for a fight.

So few can tune their ears to hear
the echoes of regret and isolation
welling behind a killer's eyes

or see how loud open mouths
too send an anguished prayer.

A Walking Apology

It wasn't the words
that broke me, it was
hijacking my healing;
for what it's worth,
when the fender bent and
crumbled so many times that
lost meaning
became all that was left
for the taking
I never asked
your forgiveness

I'm sorry
I'm sorry
I'm sorry
I'm sorry
I'm sorry
I'm sorry
I'm sorry
I'm sorry
and I'm sorry
to walk both with
and without an apology.

Dissociation Versus

I could not stop the blood from spilling
or staining everything it touched.

A vase tipped, and from inside came
everything I shouldn't have said —
what would have sounded better
spoken through my own sad mouth
or filtered through a better negotiator
than a phone screen and a suspicion.

People tell me that when I am focused
I look angry. My voice is deep
like a dirt road or a stranger
launching catcalls from corridors.

I know I am direct, even at my best.
In between bests, the arrow
sports a broader, more piercing head

but at my worst I am...

Gone:
        the part that I don't vividly recall.

I have reviewed the evidence.
Rewound the tape until it spiraled
and all I found is what I believed —

not a lie, but a microscope
focused so closely it blurred
what was hungry to be believed

more honest, or attended to
in places I'd dug caverns to conceal.

I know that I have projected
the shadows in my vision, imposed
onto what was likely innocuous or
unintentional. Absent or unclear.

I know that perception was so skewed
some thought I spoke from cruelty
instead of fear, striking first
and confirming identity later.

When the haze clears
anything I've seen lurking is...

Gone:
          the faint smell of smoke after lightning.

I could not capture the moment
I decided *I wish to consume.*

Maybe it never happened. Or maybe
starving and hunting look the same
when both equally desperate.

So many days, seeing the past
requires me to pit memory
against a mushroom cloud.
Intentions against a void.

What is an ask versus a demand?
Or a remark versus a diatribe?
Skirting accountability versus

Gone:

       the only word I have to describe it.

Submerged in the absence of clarity.
Untethered in a psychotic flood.
Dissociation versus a desire to say
this is why neither of us can trust me.

I wish I could tell you I understand
why, how, or when I lost myself
but when I came to, all I found
was an empty bed. A slain corpse

and your sad mouth, no longer
moving to inform me of my wrongs.

You do not believe I deserve
forgiveness. I believe that too —
I have to in order to sleep at night

but when I stare for too long
scowling, downturned, fangs
sharper out than they will ever be in

apologies all sound empty. Sorrys
fall in forests of broken promises
with sight-lines obscured by trees.

How many times have I penned
rants to unwilling recipients
only to see them ripped up and
returned as confetti years later?

How many words did I launch
without discretion
when rationale called in sick
and rationality clocked out early?

There are assumptions that I was right
woven into misguided tirades.
Logical leaps from dangerous heights.
Volumes raised by overwhelm's bullhorn.

My humor doused in so much pessimism
that it only ever floated in salt beds.

There are times I floored the gas
forgetting someone else was riding shotgun.

Fell asleep with my eyes open,
watching from above, appalled
and screaming at this stranger
to stop throwing out the bathwater.

I could spare sticks and stones.
Could chain myself to the lamppost.
Could choose the method of destruction,
even when the destruction began
long before fingers pointed to direct it.

I've gone further into the storm
like taking a hammer to wet paper
when all it did was tear straight through.
The sound of its impact imitating
not being dropped, but thrown.

There are things I am told I have done
and impacts I am told I have had.
There are lives I am told I have ruined
and bridges that are burning still.

I promise, if I picked up a match — struck it
knowing full well what hell it would ignite —
I would have hurled myself into a river and
baptized everything unforgivable.

Some days I wonder if that too
would have made so many waves
they consumed instead of cleansing.

So maybe this is the only truth I have

or can handle

or both.

Still, the aftermath tells me enough
that I never hesitate to plead guilty.

There was no one else in the room. They are...

Gone:
            scattered facts and shredded blessings

and I am standing over a crime scene
hands both soaked in crimson.

I might not remember what happened
but I will always admit that I did something...

...whatever it was.

Riddle

The doctor looks at me
like I have just told her
I have a thorn in my paw.

"I guess you'll just have to deal with it"

she says, after entering my symptoms
into an ancient database
for the third time this year,
still coming up empty.

I wonder how often she's used
this gas-canned dismissal

and scour her face for a clue
that she understands

how I just told her without telling her
that I have started leaving the car
running a little too long in the garage

because, like her
my options are depleted.

Her reply is a chessboard
deadlocked in a stalemate —
sterile and frozen
as the checked linoleum tiles

and after my first suicide attempt
I wonder if this is what she means
by "deal with it."

Answer:
Identifying a body

Explanation, Not Excuse

In 1995
scientists traced the root of hypertrichosis,
a type of abnormal hair growth
known as "Werewolf Syndrome,"
to extra DNA near the SOX3 gene.

> I doubt anyone ever told children
> sprouting tufts from their cheekbones
> they were making it up for attention.

In 1995
the protein leptin was injected into mice
after researchers found the genetic defect
causing them to produce excess fat cells.

> I hope the mice weren't encouraged
> to spend more time on the wheel
> and stop eating so much cheese.

In 1995
Pepcid is approved to treat heartburn.
Pig valves replace human cardiac muscle.
The first triple organ transplant is performed.

> It would be impossible to make the excuse
> that this just wasn't a good year for science.
> That medicine was still in its infancy.

In 1995
my disorder is still heavily debated.
Listed as "not otherwise specified."
Called a "culture bound syndrome."

     We have already discovered werewolves
     yet my body is still somehow a mystery.
     A genome too tightly wound to decipher.

In 2013
the DSM-5[1] upturns generations of wrongs.
Gray's Anatomy,[2] however, falls short
perhaps mistaken for a television drama[3]

     I have already spent ten years
     playing host to an unnatural plague
     before it gains a seat at the table.

In 2017
they find the culprit in the brain.
Mutations in the ESR1 and ESC/EZ genes
are marked both responsible and heritable.

     I have just lost my medical insurance.
     People tell me I really need therapy.
     I have still never heard of my disorder.

In 2023
my diagnosis is finally stamped into a file
next to my name. I read all the studies.
It was the only way to decipher a single clue.

My partner turns to me and says
You can't keep using your illness
as an excuse for everything.

In 1995, I am five years old.
I bite a kid in my kindergarten class
after he tells me that I look like a dog.

Someone asks me why I did it.

I still don't have an explanation.

---

1 The Fifth Edition of the *Diagnostic and Statistical Manual of Mental Disorders*, first published in 2013 and revised in 2022; the standard diagnostic tool for psychiatric and mental health practitioners.

2 A human anatomy reference guide written by Henry Gray in 1858; the 42nd edition released in 2020; long considered a standard text for medical students and practitioners.

3 *Grey's Anatomy* is a popular television drama series about the work (and love) lives of doctors, cleverly named for the protagonist, Meredith Grey; originally aired in 2005; renewed for its 22nd season in 2025.

Dead Language

The first mention of a werewolf was in The Epic of Gilgamesh —
an ancient tale about a hero seeking eternal life.
It is the oldest surviving story, penned in Sumerian.

Sumerian is a dead language. I cannot speak it.
It was never taught to me, like it was never taught to most.
Those who created its characters are all dead now.

The Epic of Gilgamesh is a story about death.
I know death. How to speak its language, babbling
to itself in a dark cave like a child who was raised there.

I read this story in an English class, in a small room
with a woman who wanted me to know its lessons
but far too late for it to feel either exciting or simple.

I learned the language of healing in a small room
with a woman who wanted me to know its lessons
far too late for it to feel either exciting or simple.

From me she rose a dead language. A story of the thing
I had always been, but only ever babbled to myself about.
I tripped over my tongue a thousand times. I cried.

I grieved all the wounds that I had never known.
The people I could only ever speak to in the tongue
I kept trying to bury along with the rest of me.

It took years to learn that I too was not history.
The past is the past, but the words do not have to stay
for the story to carry on, borne in a new interpretation.

I do not seek eternal life, but the caves, the paintings
and the shadows on their walls, often mistaken for my own.
I want to greet them all by name. To write their story too.

VIII
WANING

VIII
WANING

Chemistry Class

The doctors don't listen to us
so we run home to play chemistry class.
Google our way through medical school,
our own bodies the experimental mice running
mazes of wrong answers, desperate for an end.

Environments made us test tubes
like statistics make us risk factors
and they named us
after so many men in the textbooks,
but nobody ever studied our joy.

Instead, we are hypothesizing and testing
for anything resembling work-life balance
or not being in pain on most of the days
or oil-and-watering toxic burnout culture
when we are already walking explosives
trying to stand still in iron maiden DNA.

Medicine was never designed to make us well.
They only ever taught us to nurse, attend,
and listen to our hearts with stethoscopes —
no wonder the vials and syringes feel awkward
in our inexperienced hands. I could probably
diagnose an autoimmune disorder with a keyboard
at this point, but on paper there is no answer
besides Clinical. Hysteria. Gaslight. Treatable
with weight loss, Xanax, birth control, pregnancy
yoga, or *maybe just try to ignore it, Darling.*

I mean, I wouldn't be caught dead in a pussy hat,
but the worst part about having a uterus
or a body that is a puzzle with more than two pieces
is that they really are ignoring this many of us.
Misdiagnosing potentially fatal conditions
like I'd really rather hear that abject misery
can be cured by an apple a day and lifestyle changes.

So watch as we burn down the lab on purpose
because we are sick of lying at pain charts
while we scream at the sky in Morse code.

After all, if the people who are meant to help us
refuse to even see us, are we not already ghosts?

If so many are dying for an answer
we already know, why do the equations
never change to account for the invisible patients
sitting in formaldehyde jars, banging on the glass?

Can you hear us when your literature doesn't?
Can you believe us when you've been trained not to?

Because that's the only alternative to the unacceptable.

If our recourse is healing, the race to discover a cure
might just put an entire industry out of business.

Chemistry class is in session. Doctor, keep pretending
that you were asleep when they told you animals
will always evolve to increase their chances at survival.

Your formulas yielded us no solutions, so now
we are using every tool we stole from you
to save ourselves.

The Leech Doctor

(after Andrea Gibson)

The leech doctor told me
that she needed to bleed me dry

                    in order to figure out where
                    exactly the poison was.

The barber-surgeon said
she could cut my hair shorter —
take the thorns out of my paws

                    but couldn't pull out my teeth
                    or wash the blood off my hands.

The apothecarist sold me a dram.
He said it would make me happier

                    even though it just made me sleep,
                    which I guess made me happier,
                    because I didn't feel much of anything.

The general practitioner

          sent me to a gynecologist

                              who sent me to a chemist

          who sent me to an insurer

                              which sent me to a call center
                              that put me on hold until

I sent myself to the ER doctor

who sent me to an institution

which sent me to a psychiatrist

who sent me to the pharmacy

which sent me into psychosis...

The psychosis prescribed
        a strict regimen of isolation
a daily dose of self-destruction
        and enough denial to mistake
a death wish for a sense of humor.

The leech doctor told me
that if the treatment failed

I must not have given enough.

That she would take my money
but didn't want my history.

The psychologist took my history
before he assured me that
the only thing wrong with me
was that something was wrong

which meant that the parasite, not I
was what needed to be drained
until there was nothing left.

The therapist told me to keep my blood;

all she needed to help me
was a sharp knife
and an hour a week
to pry open my heart

and tear out the truth.

Operation (in Five Pieces)

1. (Broken) Heart

When I was a kid, my friends would play Operation:
the game where you use a pair of plastic tweezers
to pull objects out of holes in a human-shaped container
without touching the sides of its incisions.

If you did, it would set off an alarm, like a monitor
threatening to fail, or flutter, or flatline.

I never liked it much. It seemed too easy to make
careless mistakes with conductors awaiting sparks.
Heartbeats meant to stay perfectly steady in crisis.

The directive is meant to be simple:

Poke around for the anomalies,
in a body artificially sung electric
but don't ever nick the edges

and definitely do not kill the patient
in some whimsical desire to save them.

2.   (Adam's) Apple

My friend Molly committed suicide
our sophomore year of high school
before she could branch or bloom.
They say she was depressed before,
but word around the morgue was
that somebody tried to play pharmacist
with a pair of plastic tweezers —

I wonder if the coroner plucked out pills
like bobbing for poison apples.

When we lost Amy too, it seemed like
American pie had caved in on the windowsill.

Olivia died and they said it wasn't the trauma
that convinced her to bite off her hands,
rather the reason she stopped breathing
was the rotten fruit caught in her throat.

3.   Butterfly (in the stomach)

"Cavity Sam" as his makers called him —
the clown full of holes — knows the joke:

*Side effects may cause depression, anxiety
or thoughts of suicide.* The game masters
promise a grandiose metamorphosis.
Advertise cause and cure in the same box.

I remember being sad because I was sick
but I never wanted to die until Big Pharma
started poking around in my anatomy
like we're all two-dimensional bottom lines
lying flat on a table. Willing to let anyone
pin our wings beneath a microscope;
explain death away in a disclaimer.

4.   Wrench (in the knee)

I watch my friends play this game —
putting in objects and pulling them out again
as they have been trained to for years —
digging for answers without
the proper tools to maneuver gently.

Must be that they're professional surgeons now,
seeing no risk in holding scalpels to their wrists
inching closer every time their name
is called across a pharmacy counter.

5.   (Funny) Bone

I never really liked Operation.
We approached the body like children
brimming with joyful carelessness
nervous laughter, and low stakes.

What if we go looking for broken legs
and accidentally pull a life from its body?

What happens when we get so close to the edge
that only the shock of loss, like paddles
clinging to the chest of a corpse
can convince us that sometimes

there is little difference
between tablets in a bottle
pieces on a game board
and a single bullet, spinning
in the chamber of a gun.

The Pack

I found The Pack in a place
where all hope seemed lost.

A safe haven for imaginary friends
huddled together in chat threads;
sanctuary in the comments section.

I never knew that I could find
so much life in the same sewer
where humanity goes to decay

but this is where my limbs
started growing rosebuds
in place of frostbitten fingers.

Mycelium bridging redwoods
held candles to how deep
the roots of sadness run
through pyres razed by wolves.

Alone we were dying
but together we untethered
our leashes, wove and dropped
stronger anchors.

Remembered that
even in the times
we weren't believed,
or believed in, we were still
so unbelievably brave.

Chasing Our Tails

(after Solmaz Sharif)

Have you tried
Prozac? Iron supplements
fortified with honey

from free-range bees?
Blood of an infant who has
never known true sadness
mixed in your green tea

with a Vegan breakfast?
Meditating in an intersection?
Intracranial massage? Have you

journaled while screaming?
Danced through sleep paralysis
with your face contorted into a grin?

Or tried giving up? Letting the pain
swallow the rest of you?
Doom spiraled into

consequences like a plane
accepting inevitable free-fall?
Have you told your inner child
to take some paid time off?

Are you irritable?
Unable to function?
Have you sometimes wondered
if living isn't really for you?

And have you consulted with
every medical expert in the country
about your condition? All of them?

Sung to yourself in a staff meeting?
Overwhelmed your support system?
Taken another Midol? Have you

looked yourself in the mirror
and tried to love someone

you don't recognize anymore?
Have you considered running

in circles until you become
a black hole? Which program

do you follow? What guru
do you see? Whose tail
are you chasing?

Amends

1. Broken Nucleotide Pairs
(or A Censored List of People I Have Loved and Lost Without Closure)

C — c
   R — y
      N — e   D — e
         R — t   K — e
                                J — e
           A — e   R — e
           L — a   C — n
           T — y   J — y
                C — n   S — f   A — n
           B — t   O — a
         S — h   J — n
      J — n   H — h
   A — o   S — e
   J — e   J — e
   N — s   A — y
   S — a   C — a
A — y   L — h

                                          & The Person I Was
                                          Before All of Them

2. On Grief

I live in a graveyard.
This is the fault of either
my actions or theirs.
Or death. Or gravity.

Some are still alive.
Some are dead and buried
and some are just buried
in brimming chasms of reverie.

The love was not always love.

Sometimes it was need or
coincidence, or a fleeting way
to feel more alive in light
of so many apparitions, but loss
is loss no matter if or where
the body is interred. So many
of these bodies were broken
by the ghost in my body.

So much grief birthed new
grief: children of absence.

The left breeding fear of leaving.
The harlequin turning tricks
for an abandoned carnival,
empty as a hurricane's eye.

Now, Grief is my shepherd.
God left this place long ago.

I walk down rows of angels
forever trapped in stone
and imagine their names
are the lines of a poem.

3\. Unraveling is Not A Revision
(or What I Wish I Would Have Said)

This isn't love,
but I miss you
like an unfinished kiss
or life ended too soon,
even through the bondage
that could have stayed pure
proving the heart is clearly
mistaking fear for spite
and your disappearance
when I wanted you most
wasn't a betrayal of trust
but rewriting closeness —
a glass house of ambiguity,
built on crumbling stones
after quiet resentment
destroyed us both

because you scare me,
like laughter after a kill,
shot at a sewn-on shadow
relishing in forced shame,
that imposes cruelty &
uncoils angry silence
volatile enough to retaliate
when I was running away
into something like death
& the inability to evolve
— I am not falling apart
if you can see me standing,
charting an upward spiral
spinning gold from dirt
and all your demons
by rewinding the past

& sometimes the beauty of retrospect
is how it won't let us pretend
that we aren't still human.

Clipping

I have always been a composer — a songbird
afraid of having my wings clipped...

Sometimes I look to the clouds and hear music.
Sometimes I pick up on the racing baseline pulse
beneath a stranger's voice when they speak.
Sometimes I can trace the strings between ideas
like a score full of held notes, delicately interwoven
every beat laid out in a profound symphony.

I've never wanted to lose the beauty through
the dust of hurt and disappointed aftermath
after triggering the richter-scale detonation
of an atomic bomb buried in Eden — I know
that rose colored glasses see no red flags
but without them, what would I have left to love?
What can I hold in my hands when major keys
start to sand-grain slip through my fingers?

In music, they call the sensation clipping:
When a sound has outgrown its housing.
When it is too big, too deeply felt, too dramatic
for machines or human ears to receive it easily.
It is something you are supposed to avoid.
Something that must be turned down
for the song to remain even
or palatably contained.

Sound engineers use equalizers to ensure
none of the instruments clip in the final mix —
that it follows a standard statistical curve,
normalized with every outlier muted down.

I have always been a songbird — a composer
afraid of having my wings clipped...

...but my world becomes too loud.
The air punches instead of glides and
all of those big, beautiful crescendos
become death by a thousand cacophonies
a dissonant, grating scream in place of song
an out-of-sync orchestra with too many tempos...
a composition of mostly car horns and snare drums
and sopranos whistling tones into the rafters
shaking years of careful architecture to ruin.

They told me that mood stabilizers would clip the ends.
That the trebles and basses would become a little less bright
but so would the lightning strikes and thunder claps.

The melodies would lose their luster, but so would the bullets
and the shattered glass when I cannot hold up
the fragility of my skin against every flash flood
that rushes through in violent, crashing waves.

I knew they were working when the tempo slowed
and each thought's buzzing accompaniment
became an adjustable sound wave.

The bleating choir of a body keeping too many scores
capable of being turned up... or down... or off... at will.
A type of refrain I never thought I'd be skilled enough
to perform without a thousand incidentals...

Maybe I can't fly as close to the sun anymore.
Maybe this means no mortal was meant to.

Maybe I can be satisfied instead with the tools
to engineer suspension. If the quiet makes me honest

enough to hear a pin drop in the forest, my wings
have been broken for so long that I lost faith in flight,
like trying to pilot a life from the fiery cockpit
of a pipe dream filled with jet fuel and feathers.
I have always been afraid of having my wings clipped

but I am aloft for the first time in a while now.

I can still hear the music, but it doesn't hurt anymore.
It is simple, controlled, and beautiful

like the ring of a single violin
rising slowly —
delicately —
into the sunrise.

XIX
NEW

XIX

Kintsugi

(after Cadence McCracken)

In the cracks   I   am so lucky to have barely found
the strength to   heal   the monster that broke me
and almost destroyed   every   hard-earned monument
erected by spending   time   to grow a garden
root by root, seed   by   seed; my worth
is the bulb just barely   starting   to bloom again
I hope it grows to reach   over   my head.

A Break Up Letter

1. To The Wolf

This is not a warning.
This is a coffin nail.
A stake through both stigmata.
An excavation of suffering.

I no longer agree to feed you.
To let you live comfortably in this body
with two extra rows of teeth
and a shadow three sizes too big
for one who was not born for the hunt.

Each small white tablet is a moon
capable of eclipsing your slaughter.
Your greatest power is mine now.
I heal by charting a new astronomy.
Scheduling weekly exorcisms.

You will die and I will not follow you there.
My days will dawn and dawn and dawn
and still, yours will never have begun.

2. From The Wolf

You are only free because I let you go.
Therefore, you are never truly free.

A mask is not a rebellion any more
than I am a momentary departure.
It is said that I only become stronger,
but silver bullets don't come cheap.

How long until each chip in your resolve
brings you back to me, panting for air?
Thirsty for blood? Howling my name?

There will be a day that I vanish,
but a part of you will vanish with me.
The one that calls itself warrior, saint —
wears my head on its sword...
and all you will be left with is silence.

Will you still dream about me?
Will I be strongest as a memory?

Or when the night becomes safe again
what will you do with all of that peace?

When There is Only Sun

When the night stops descending
and the massive round pull in the night
becomes a pebble in the pale blue of noon.

When this is the only form of weather left
I wonder if I imagined it all.

If the fiction was in The Turning
or in so drastic a shift in cosmic order.

I never thought we could exist without nighttime.
I thought the moon was a constant body
left invisible over the horizon.

I do know that she still lives, but in the way
the spirits of the departed linger, eyes lie
and the dead have no mouths.

I cherish this kind of hopeful delusion.
This irresponsible optimism.
I have not seen the Goddess Nocturne
fall from the sky in months now.

I wonder if I ever slept to save daylight.
I wonder if I turned time's hands back to extend
the hours in which I governed my own orbit.

The moon once ruled my calendar.
Now I miss staring into her sad, beautiful face.

She appears to me a reverie. A storybook.
A fantasy I made up to justify so much darkness:
that little, defiant speck of hope.

Now that the only shadows are bright
and diamond-encrusted and burning
I can only imagine the atmosphere
being a reflection. A glimpse.

But what about the night?
Did it have any meaning of its own?
Was the hand of some higher power
right to banish it entirely?

I wrote so many poems after sunset.
2AM was both the chasm and the spring.
Mornings for finding art arranged in chaos's bed.

Which well do I draw from now?
What void can I stare down to feel
anything blinking back is a miracle?

How does one envy the stars —
a colony of destructions —
when they've prayed to the dirt
to stop moving beneath them?

Have I banished dusk to misery?
Outlawed the witching hour? Murdered the Muse?
Will the three ghosts refuse to visit me
because they have no space left to plant growth?

Could I be saved if the sin is removed for me?

I ask these questions, but feel no shame.
I can't stomach any more than what I do not need
and I do not need a small rock's tragedies.

Still, I have never wanted this badly
to need a flashlight
squinting to see in the dark.

To praise the moon
or even thank her
for guiding me all this way
to unending morning.

Fixed

I stood still, spinning in a pattern
of codons, winding downward,
watching the merry-go-round
of prismatic galloping and laughter
rotate, lights flickering on and off
while days and nights passed, and I
lived in the perpetual eye of the storm

for twenty-two trips around the sun

the world kept turning without me and the world kept turning without me and
the world kept turning without me and the world kept turning without me and
the world kept turning without me and the world kept turning without me and
the world kept turning without me and the world kept turning without me and
the world kept turning without me and the world kept turning without me and
the world kept turning without me and the world kept turning without me and
the world kept turning without me and the world kept turning without me and
the world kept turning without me and the world kept turning without me and
the world kept turning without me and the world kept turning without me and
the world kept turning without me and the world kept turning without me and
the world kept turning without me and the world kept turning without me

and suddenly...
I started to turn with it...

arms uncoiling from the machinery
as they invited me to join the parade
I had only ever watched pass by

like a daydream orbiting a void.

I am still dizzy, vomit-soaked and
head-aching, wondering if bewilderment
was the only favor handed out
at the party I'd shown up late for

or if I would have found my sea-legs
further in the past — bitten through
the cage bars, so rabid for joy
that I broke my jaw — I would
be dancing a platformed ballet by now
with all the other pretty horses —

instead of questioning why it seems
so much easier to stagnate, gear-stuck
than to untangle every wire, spooled
and interlaced around my history
like I was mummified alive while the circus
looked on in horror, or amusement

or why some days I wonder if it would have
been safest to remain TV static and tightly
wound, held in the stasis of being broken

than to ferry the nauseous, whimsical burden
of reinventing the carousel of memories
and reclaiming what it means to be fixed.

Normal

After six months of treatment
that looked more like a cure
than a landslide of backsteps

I wrote my name over and over
just to make sure it looked
the same each time.

I sat on hillsides and watched
as the night came and went.

Photographed my fingers
pointing at constellations
so they could never shift.

This life is beautiful now —
It doesn't mean I'm not terrified.

Degeneration is still my prognosis
just as much as the trauma
has wrapped itself around
every too-fast pulse

but I think this must be
what normal feels like:
one hand on the door latch
and two feet on the ground.

I repair instead of ruin.
I hold tight and don't let go.

I am safe now. I can love
with the cell door open.

Phoenix

When I met myself at the end of all of it
we spoke about what we had seen together

watching me try to get back
to the person we both knew
I was all along — trying to hold
a loving home for them while
they flailed and disintegrated
in mirror pools of poisoned mud.

I look back at this younger iteration
and wonder if we should take
who cowered in a corner for years
to allow her to share our name.

People say a lot about what it is to be sick,
but they talk little of how hard it is to be well
when wellness cloaks its face. Sometimes

I look in the rearview, see my eyes
virtue-clear, and wonder if they are lying.

Still presenting an oasis that might shortly
fizzle to dunes. I would ask no one
to believe that this calm is permanent.

I've become accustomed to anomalies.
Short reprieves between tempests.

For a time, it was healthiest
to believe myself flickering
waste. Better off absent
or someone else's problem.

I am not afraid of this anymore

though still shiver at the the belief
that progress is just gold-plated failure.
That any hill-and-dip, spiraling path
is a journey of a thousand backsteps.

A sick body without medicine is dying
and a vacant heartbeat can resurge
with the lightning of reanimated flesh

but if it flatlines and no one believes
it will flap its wings again, it won't.

I decry the amateur morticians claiming
the only rest for the wicked is in soil

so I am dragging this cadaver upstream
bloated, drowned, and still breathing —

this sunken-faced seraphim —
faith I feared downed in flight
billowing from the soot pile

and I love her
and I have missed her so much

since we found seeds
where the earth was salted
in fields razed by a stone cold tiller.

Healing came from the bottom
of a barrel of broken promises
and time of death declared.

So if I stayed
it was because I chose to
and if I burned bridges,
it was to teach
my singed feathers to fly solo.

So even if you would have waited
for the chapel's carved spires to topple
before filling a single pew

I commit to rejoicing —
blowing out the candles rekindled
without the offer of flint or tinder.

Marvel at this salvaged life:

a triumph once believed
to be little more
than a wake.

And All I Have Lost

And at some point, I started counting bodies
And I saw myself lying among them
And I wondered what that makes me now

And I embraced the monster in the mirror
And I knew that every flicker of goodness
      had no bearing on a mass of bystanders
And a version of myself that isn't so ferocious
      lived outside of most common understanding
And I saw myself just through their eyes:
      as violence seeking flesh. As hunger
      for softness in the midnight feast

And where this shame thrives
      the pattern repeats itself

And the memories of harm provoke harm
And I stop blaming the moon and start
      blaming the morning for trying to prove
      the possibility of restoring all I have lost

And all werewolves are werewolves because
      they were bitten by what they have become
And we are always the first victims in the story:
      children, unafraid to walk in the forest at night
And that is what I was once, before the horror
      of one savage moment became nonfiction

And I put wilted flowers on their gravestones
And I bid them farewell in the moments
      that the turning feels predestined
And I blow kisses to everyone who runs

And I understand. I am afraid of me too
And I know the carnage I am capable of

       but sometimes the past extends open palms

And forgiveness blooms a miracle from stone
And one fearless act rewrites an era
And a hushed wind whispers *I see you still*
And the shards of bone reassemble
And the pitchforks go back in the garden sheds
And the torches were never lit to begin with
And the bodies begin to take deep breaths
And my gaping jaw sews itself shut

And the bloodlust feels ancient and foreign
And the holes in the ground fill with grief
And the magic of this metaphor disintegrates
       into a sick body in an even sicker society

And the werewolf doesn't die in the end
And all the creatures retreat into hiding
And the fairy tale slams itself shut
And the author lives on as something else

because of all I have lost, not all is lost

And when the clouds part ways like old friends
And dawn tears itself open to greet me, I can see
that the best parts of me survived

because there is still something left here
worth saving

Reason

        Why
are the images drawn in my skin
all testaments to lifted veils?

do wounds teach cinched throats to splay?

is this assemblage — all battered, burned
and unburied — so reasonably brash?

is singing the alchemy of the scream?

do grief and pride both still resemble
once-estranged gears clicking to rhythm?

        Why
has my whole life led me here
to teach me what it means to love it

both before and beyond

its bitterness crumbles
into the hungry jaw
of a sweeter demolition?

Eulogy

The wolf will never die.

Skin will always run thick
with the blood of what innocence
was marked to seek destruction.

This is not a tragedy.

The tragedy is the diary
devoid of torch-singed pages

the memoirs of those
who played the game
of seeker and sought
until the slaughter was over
or the bullets ran out.

Their stories resound, quaking
like rift-pocked geography

and I do not blame them
for wanting retreat
into cryptography and myth

or banish any future
for a species facing extinction.

So instead of a eulogy
we can write them
an alternate becoming —

sing their sanguine praises
so we might someday
revere all cacophonies
barking at the wild blue

consider that requiem
Judgement's scales learning
to live among them

or learning to live
among the them
that live among us

like I have had to learn
to live among the them
that lives within me

and we can live
among the them that live
within all of us:

the memories and the monsters.

The grief and the gravity.

The madness and the miracle
never separate, only

acknowledged
loved
integrated
validated
examined

in any beholder's eyes.

There is always an ending
in which we do not die
and neither do the parts
that we wish would

and in that conclusion
every creature belongs.

So believe the werewolf
when they cry Human
through the engravings
of teeth and time —

or when they tell you
in the barest of words

that it would be
an honor and a pleasure
to meet your demons

exactly where you are

beneath the rising breath
of the next full moon —

period.

Acknowledgements

First and foremost, I want to acknowledge everyone who has believed in this collection, including everyone who this book is ultimately for. It is one thing to tell your story; it is an entirely different beast to accept that it is a story worth sharing.

Thank you to everyone who has contributed to this book in the form of reading, editing, artwork, and/or book design: J. Brandon Loberg, Martin Whitmore, Bridger Rodman, Zoe Willats, Cadence McCracken, RoseJean Weller, Mira Weller, Maxwell Folk, Jo Thompson-Parupia, Amber Romano, Rachael Smith and, of course, Kae Johnson.

A shout out to my queer and disabled communities, as well as all of the helpers, healers, artists, activists, teachers, students, leaders, and lovers who constantly remind me that this work is never done as much as it is rarely done alone. Special thanks to those who hold me in this work: my ever-inspiring colleagues (of whom there are too many), the ever-faithful collage of renegades at 16th and Mission, everyone in the Resilient Voices Poetry Group, and the blessed spiritual haven that is MDUUC.

Endless gratitude to my devoted team of doctors, nurses, therapists, and specialists who have worked tirelessly and compassionately as the stewards of my wellness. I am so lucky to have found the kind of support that I believe everyone deserves.

So much love to my family. I am proud to have been raised by wolves. It has been an honor to grow, and keep growing, alongside you. Also, to the friends who have stuck by me through every step of this journey and beyond; I know it isn't always easy, but you inspire me to always see what is still good through what is imperfect.

For those that are no longer in my life because I was not able, or willing, to keep you here: I have forgiven all that either pulled, or pushed, you away. I am sorry. I am humbled. I appreciate every opportunity for grief to be my guide.

Finally, utmost gratitude to Melissa Allen, Elisabeth Andreason, and SerasStreams, without whom this book would never see the light of day.

Thank you for your faith in me.

Resources & Further Reading

MENTAL HEALTH & WELLNESS

988 Suicide & Crisis Hotline

National Alliance of Mental Illness (NAMI)

The Trevor Project

American Foundation for Suicide Prevention (AFSP)

The Jed Foundation (JED)

We've Been Too Patient by L.D. Green and Kelechi Ubozoh

REPRODUCTIVE & SEXUAL HEALTH

Planned Parenthood

Rape, Abuse, and Incest National Network (RAINN)

PREMENSTRUAL DISORDERS

International Association for Premenstrual Disorders (IAPMD)

The Christina Bohn Foundations

National Association for Premenstrual Syndromes (NAPS)

The Cycle by Shalene Gupta

SELF HELP & STORYTELLING

The Other Side of Change by Maya Shankar

It Didn't Start with You by Mark Wolynn

Braving the Wilderness by Brene Brown

The Body is Not An Apology by Sonya Renee Taylor

You Better Be Lightning by Andrea Gibson

A Slight Change of Plans Podcast

TRAUMA, GRIEF, & HEALING

The Body Keeps the Score by Bessel Van der Kolk

The You're Going to Die: The Podcast

www.ingramcontent.com/pod-product-compliance
Lightning Source LLC
Chambersburg PA
CBHW010430120726
47992CB00010B/3395